Reject Me, Kindly

Poems on Feeling, Healing, and All the Rest

by Ayva Dupont

DORRANCE
PUBLISHING CO
EST. 1920
PITTSBURGH, PENNSYLVANIA 15238

Dorrance Publishing Co
585 Alpha Drive
Suite 103
Pittsburgh, PA 15238
Visit our website at *www.dorrancebookstore.com*

ISBN: 979-8-88925-155-2
eISBN: 979-8-88925-655-7

Reject Me, Kindly

Poems on Feeling, Healing, and All the Rest

For
the Heartbroken

unconsciously conscience

i choose to fill my narrative
of loneliness
by selecting people who are
emotionally unavailable

i cry myself to sleep
because the seed in my head
sprouts from wet pillow

if i can predict that you will leave
perhaps it might hurt less
but i'm a known emotional masochist

love deprived

in the last life
i would have shriveled
from the drought
that you brought

on grainy palms
i would crawl
across dunes
sand whipping in face
stinging red eyes
thirsting for the sweet sound
of your approval

i would look for
pools of empathy
where there is none
a mirage of your love
desolate

but in this life,
i will dig until water
puddles at my hands
because i cannot wait
for your rain shower
mere trickles in hot sky

you are not the only source
to fill me full
and i will not tire myself
into the convincement
that you are

feelings

i let your kisses ferment
on my forehead
but they have grown stale
because you are here
and so am i
but i have wept
salty oceans
trying to convince you
of the validity of my feelings
for you to not know
if you have any

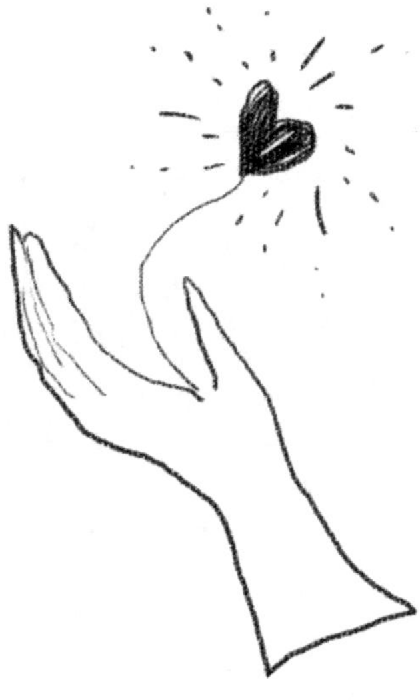

we don't want to part ways

i will give you my heart
over and over again
i will play devil's advocate
pulling rope from each side
of my mind
until there is a clear winner:
the determinant of
whether i should tell you
that i love you
or not
i'm not ready for this to end
and i know you aren't either
let me cry in your shoulder
in preparation
for never seeing you again
i hope we find each other
when timing is better

situationship

i grieve over the person
who was never mine
the one who told me
their innermost thoughts
dressed in an intimacy
that i had never experienced.
lovers without feeling
but when severed
i wanted nothing but you
how confusing it is that when
we decided to just be friends
i wanted more

emotionless

i have tried to love you whole
your heart
petrified rock
i wish to chisel and soften
through peephole,
i see glimpses of
your potential
you could be so wonderful
and we could be so happy
but i cannot do
the work for the both of us.
i will not sacrifice myself
for the cause
of freeing you
from a misery you choose

the east and west wall

i'm not mad at you
we didn't end bitterly
sugar didn't boil until burn
i have no poor feelings
toward you

sometimes i wish we fought
until we felt cheeks turn
hot to touch
red with rage

but the truth is
there was no turning point
in time
where i second guessed us
where i doubted us as a compound

you didn't call me names
or sleep on the couch
one day we started facing
opposite walls

the needle never points to
east and west
at the same time
meanwhile our bodies split
tectonic plates sliding

we were just complacent
and we both deserved more

far apart

i like to think that
maybe
just maybe
you and i are looking
at the same freckled sky
at the same time;
you were always good
at pointing out
the constellations

to love my soul and not just my body

i say that i do not want
someone right now
but what i really mean is
i do not want the heat
from a body
tangled in the sheets
to dissipate when the
covers are lifted

i do not want to be
someone's temporary pleasure
whose voice is only good
when laid in their ear
but instead to be loved in a capacity
in which i cannot fully know
because the edges are blended
as our bodies spill
into each other

and i do not want to
be loved in the dark
i am better than that

so when i say i do not want
someone right now
what i really mean is

i want someone
but the same someone
that touches my skin
to also peel back my layers
unravel my core
and cradle my vulnerability:

climb into me
and touch my insides

ravenous

ravenous is your appetite
for my shame.
you pick a part my skin
tear open my flesh
and butterfly my ribcage.
what a glorious feast
it must be
to feed off someone
who knows no boundaries
because they have been conditioned
to give you everything
in exchange for nothing

i am not a hopeless romantic

i am not a hopeless romantic

no.

perhaps the word hopeless is fitting though
because i find myself more and more withered
each time a love fails

i am not a hopeless romantic

no.

but i want someone to remember
the way i like my coffee:
somewhere between lukewarm and barely warm at all
the cheaper, the better
especially when not prepared by myself

i want someone to know my favorite color too
because it emulates my personality
but it's no longer yellow
perhaps a dull gray from all the times
i've asked questions
to never be explored in return

i used to be a hopeless romantic

yes.

longing to be one of two barn swallows

chasing tail in the
sunrise sky in late april
when the air nips bitter
but smells sweet of fresh earth emerged

i thought that if i manifested hard enough
someone would make me feel seen
but really i've been on a carousel of disappointment
"you'll find it when you least expect it."

at this point,
i've been battered by past lovers
who have stripped me from the expectation of
finding something meant just for me

i am not a hopeless romantic
no.

and if i tell this to myself enough,
maybe i'll exhaust myself
into the acceptance that
love is not for everyone
and surely not for me

i fell for the idea

i've been mourning someone
that i didn't actually know
—the feeling of authenticity
a touch on my skin
that prickles into my spine
and the voice of calm
that has awakened my senses
i fell for the idea of someone
based on the person they presented
i fell for the feeling
of being held
not skin to skin
but soul to soul
as i beared secrets that i had
barely found courage to utter to myself
and how am i supposed to
let go of someone
who made me feel like sunshine
how am i to grieve
when you left
with pieces of my identity
my stories
and now i do not feel like me

sheets

i haven't changed the sheets
since the last time you were here
some time ago
because i am afraid to wash away
the last remnant of you
a crinkle in the cotton
from your body impression
and washing them
would make it feel real
when i am not yet ready
to let go of you

offering

my hands are cracked
not from this december air
but from this skin of porcelain
that attempts to protect me
from the feeling of loss

after you beckon me into bed
i extend my palms upward to you
heart in hands
because you tell me you like me

you change your mind though
from the time that my name leaves
your parted lips
to the time that i hug the sheets close
to [my] chest after parting legs

the air is cold and the hopper is empty
the last embers singe red
your heart is still beating fast
but suddenly you don't like me as much

i run stale like the air
embers now ash
you stare at the ceiling
and i worry about the way my naked
body looks in the moonlight
that spills through the windowpane
you do not want me so much now

i know i won't see you again
and mourn what could be from
the stranger that is
sharing my bed in the now
trampled heart
cracked hands
from offering myself to men
who are good at pretending

second choice

i wonder if you still think of me
when you are laying next to her
you told me you were unhappy
and i did not want to persuade you
to pursue a connection
that was not wanted.
i let you devour the idea of me
ask me why she does not taste the same
but i will not entertain your confusion
it is not fair to her nor i
and i will not be the poison
that makes you sick for a love
that you wish to deny

this was never going to last

i always knew we were temporary
but i never thought
it would hurt this much
the idea of our existence
separate
wishing each other happiness
without each other
to celebrate
that happiness
i've never hated endings more
than when i knew
we were one of them

prayer unheard

stained glass
in the cathedral
dancing light on the far wall
colors and colors
as i sit and pray
that you love me back.
you are my place of worship
i put you on a pedestal
while i cry
unheard.
what have i done
to have gone unloved
when all around me
i see belonging
oh what i would give
to experience that too

Unnamed

Vulnerability is hard
But if it were easy
I would love everybody

what happens at home

i rehearse our lives
in my head
finetune the audio
so that it fits the script
i have created
you and i look so happy
when we are not fighting
but when we are
you are so, so angry

my leaver

my legs used to quiver
at the sound of your voice,
the way you said my name
like you were the creator of it
enunciating each syllable
as its own entity

my skin used to prickle at the
thought of your touch
the idea of your fingertips mapping
constellations across the
nape of my neck
cascading down my spine
and finding home in the
divots of my lower back

how my eyes would twinkle
when yours locked with mine
and your breath ran ragged
as you whispered sweet nothings
into my skin
staining my body with words
that i do not wish
to wash away

i ache to remember the feeling of you
the one that made me feel like me
but yet, you were less man
and more Trojan Horse
as you disguise yourself as my lover
just to be my leaver

un-

i do not know how to unlearn you
but if i did
i would unfeel your lips to my collarbone
i would untether the gravity
of the earth to the sun
and unattach this impossible feeling
of my body belonging to yours.
however
i am still orbiting you
like i do not know anything else
and given the choice,
i would choose to unlove you each time

starved

i have been starved of your attention
when i have offered you nothing but mine
i have indulged you in my thoughts
making my availability an abundance that
you have devalued
because the supply is high
and here i am offering it yet again
on a silver platter
when i, myself, am emaciated

mixed signals

does he love me,
does he love me not?
it sounds less childish
as i crash into another
who does not know
how to communicate
anything but mixed signals
because his feelings are muddy
and now i am crying
begging for him to tell me
he loves me not
so that i can at least
decapitate this daisy
eat her whole
and grow a reciprocal love
for someone else to water in me

indifferent

you have lost the light in your eyes
when you look at me
i can hear them glaze over dull
when your voice comes
through the receiver
and though i cannot see your face
i know that i no longer excite you
how it stings to want someone
who has become indifferent [to you]

dirty

i feel dirty when he touches me
the way that you did
because he may please
my senses
but it is not the familiarity of you
and i am trying to reconcile
with my mind
pleading for it not to
reject someone who
is willing to give me
all of the things
that i begged you for
would he feel right to my body
if dressed in your scent?
if his voice purred the way
that yours did?
and it is not fair that i am
intertwined with someone
right now
but all i can think about is you
and i feel dirty
and want to shower
his touch down the drain
with these suds of betrayal
but then i remember
that your touch
did not want to stay

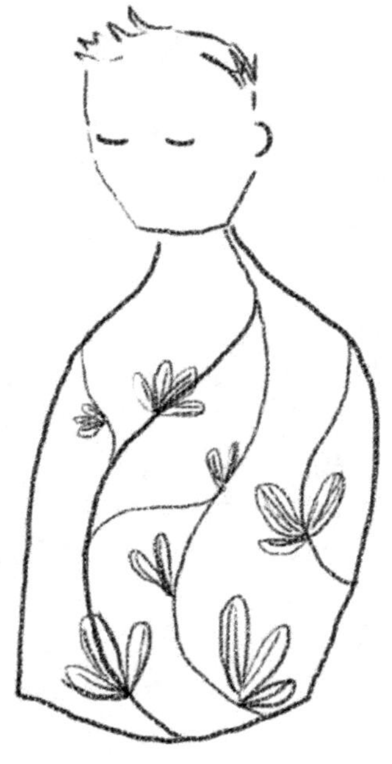

goodbyes

goodbyes are complicated
because we do not know how to
process the crested waves
of pain
and loss
and confusion.

we assume it to be somewhere between
linear and a folded fitted sheet
stored neatly in the closet
on the top shelf

and i could say goodbye
but i would spill
and now there is no one to clean me up

how do i grieve someone
whose heart is still beating
without the memory of
mine making it skip?

reject me, kindly

it is worse to give you all of me
at your convenience
when you have made it clear
that you are not consistent
and yet i offer myself
again and again
hoping that you'll look at me
in the way that you first did.
i used to pray that you would love me
and now i pray that you reject me
so that my heart can be convinced
of what my head has known all along
please kill me quickly
not with these mixed signals
of uncertainty

no one home

perhaps i broke my own heart
from living in a place
too cold to provide shelter
you watched me freeze
lips turned blue
i held myself
outside the gate of you
but your lights were off
no one to answer
so i waited until frozen
hoping you'd pry my heart
from this cold dead chest
the one that you neglected

preference

perhaps i'm a hopeless romantic
but oh the paradox
because it took me three days to process
that that the half-empty glass
of chardonnay
finding home on my nightstand
would be the last evidence of you
i'm at peace with the parting
but i would be lying
if i said that a part of me
didn't want to find way back
to each other when timing gave us
preference
so yes.
i must be a hopeless romantic

unnamed

i gargle cough syrup
choke it down
but it still hurts:
crying over you

paper

she has raised ridges
ones that show wear and texture
beautiful creases that cannot be straightened
folded by hands that are unforgiving
once origami
now crumpled paper

destruction

he is a minefield
long grass with carefully hidden explosives
disguised as a beautiful meadow
safe to collapse into
only to find yourself obliterated
into pieces

phosphenes

sometimes i don't know
if you were ever real
i see the silhouette of you
poised on pedestal
[i] give you vertebrae stairs
until i break my back
now you are so high
that i cannot see you
i rub my eyes
phosphenes
no evidence of you left
but my spine still aches

i don't want to leave you

i talk myself into the belief
that i do not care because
better things are for me
unopened doors ahead
but i like the house attached
to the one i just left
brass doorknob
laughing chimney
i know i need this door closed
but it's hard to leave you
please just evict me

numb

the hardest part about
being a numb person
is that it is perfectly selective

some days i can choose to love you
in the way that you chew your food
how you become more
shovel than person

and other days i am indifferent
and perhaps not to you
but to the way the clouds shift
from pale white to golden cream
as the sun sleeps
a rest that i too
wish my soul could take

and i miss taking a moment of awe
to recognize the beauty in the sky
something that used to excite me

but today i am numb
and i wish this was not the case
but something in me has turned off
and you choose to stay

and the hardest part about this
is that i can see the way that you
light your candle
fire feeding wick
while your innards melt first

until you become less and less
so that you can warm me

and though i am numb
i feel your love
and know it is not fair

petrichor

i don't wish to be
your maybe
when i am sweet rainfall
petrichor
during the month of april
let me water your limerence
with the susurrous of my lips
to your skin
let me prickle
hair on end
i am nothing less
than a definite
so let me be your
definitely

rot

some days i cannot
put how i feel into words
when i think of you i am not bitter
but toward one thing
you see, i made the mistake of
pouring myself into you
twisting my body to fit your mold
excusing your poor behaviors
and justifying your words of hate

i used to think that i was the problem
until i realized that this was a reflection
of your inner dilemma
because you had realized long ago that you
were not good enough
to be with a woman as strong as me

so you sought to destroy her
hoping that by dismantling her soul
you could steal her pieces
to feed your starved ego;
with greedy fingers you devoured her
chewed her
spit her out

but yet i am not bitter
but toward one thing:
how i had betrayed the woman i was
and here i am
feeling sorry for your emaciated state
because i chose to feed myself
instead of you

i hope you wither.
i hope you rot.

strangers

i do not know how i should feel
or if there is a name to this tightness
burrowing into my chest
my deepest secrets used to
seep into your skin
and i cannot undo this like you:
unfasten our conversations
whispered in the dark
when the rest of the world was sleeping

and i have recognized
that you have started
to slip from my fingers
and i'm desperately cupping you
but you are water
and fall through the spaces
between my knuckles
the gap between my fingers

and it has been weeks in which we
speak less and less
and today you told me
that you miss hearing from me
as if we are now strangers

meanwhile, i do not know
how i should feel
now that my reality has been validated
can we go back?

self-betrayal

i am disappointed in myself
i have watered my own roots
spritzed my own leaves
and created an ideal environment
for me to flourish in
yes, i have grown into myself
but then you
a japanese beetle
slid under the crack of the door
and told me you were hungry.
i should have told you no
but instead i let you consume all of me
because only then would you be satisfied
and in retrospect
if i could do this all over again
i would have honored my worth
and befriended pesticide

woodworker

i wish you to know me
edge to edge
all the messy
the thoughts in my head
the feelings that are fleeting
then maybe you could restore them
be my maker
carve art out of my insides
and blow the dust off my brittle bones

pixels

i long to be loved
not in the dark
not at 2am
not in pixels
that arrange themselves
on my screen
i long to be loved
in the light of day
because that is what i deserve

what we had

i cannot remember
a time in which i loved myself
and yet they tell me
i cannot love another
until i love myself
and this is simply not true
because they do not know
how my heart danced
when i was with you

permanent

some days i am perplexed
by the number of faces i see
the names i know
the voices i have committed to memory
and i wonder
if i too have been made permanent
in someone else's mind

that long text

i should not wage war with words
because i have fought with my thoughts
and laid them out
in front of you
strategically chosen so that
we could wave a white flag
i simply want you to understand
how you have hurt me
and though i am tempted
to write and write
a novel that you will never read
i don't
because i know that you already know
all the ways that you have hurt me
and yet, you don't care
i will not waste my time
on someone emotionally illiterate

my answer

it is sad that you once gave me
every star in the sky
collected in your arms
simply because you believed that
i was to be your only compass.
and here we are now
and i am begging you
for your attention
when all i have been given is your silence
and i ask you if you still have feelings
if you could please just tell me
if they have fled.
if they have fled.
if they have feld.
tonight i saw all the stars rearranged
across the horizon

martyr

he is eager to drag her name
as if he were martyr to a connection
that he faked
when she died over and over
for a love that she thought
was real

love crumbs

i have let myself down
too many times
hoping that you have realized
that i've been what you've
been wanting all along
but each time i am greeted
with disappointment
as you toss your love crumbs to me
knowing that i am starving
and resting at your feet
waiting to snatch any bits that i can
must i beg?

too much

they say that i feel too much.
they tell me this like i am sour
so perhaps i am an acquired taste
but tell me
when did caring for another
become too much?

naive

i told you that i was afraid you'd hurt me
and you whispered that you wanted
nothing more than to keep me safe.
was it crueler that you had manipulated
my feelings to get
what you had wanted?
or was it that i had
let myself believe you?

plastic bag

grief is a weird thing
one day you wake up fine
the sun is shining
the sky is open
you can breathe when the act
of breathing seemed impossible
then the next
it swallows you
like you are choking on your own air
and you are left wondering
when the plastic bag will be
removed from your face

black welt

i have been burned by lovers
who wanted to warm me
but did not know how to.
singe my skin
let me crisp
black. black welt.

you cheat

it is a normal response
to be angry at a betrayal
i did not tie your hands
behind your back and force you
to be an unwilling participant
in a catastrophic plot twist
no.
while you sit here and cry
puddles of salt tears
on my lap
dampening my corduroy skirt
begging me not to leave
you tell me it is all her fault.
and it is a normal response
to be angry at a betrayal,
i'll say this until you hear it,
because you shift accountability
and make it another woman's problem.
she owes me nothing.
you however,
you are the collateral

i can't let go

you knocked and i answered
as i always do
is it your expectation or mine
that i will forever be here
waiting for you?

for the complicated
thoughts & feelings

lit

i blame others for lighting me on fire
when i am made of kindle and
hand them a lit match
but arson never looked so good

to: the green

i think that you are too green
and it makes me envy
because you spill healthy
and i am waiting for it bleed
red
on the floor

inside my head tells me to stop
because i do not trust
my judgment anymore
and the way you hold your word
makes me think that it is waiting
to shatter;

if you hand it off to me
i just might drop it
to prove a point:

i cannot trust you
because all i know is
that i may be loved in the now
but tomorrow you may see
the cracks

you, the green flag
do not want me
who has been stained
red by broken promises

my thoughts, the spider

i've spent all this time
spinning a thought
grooming myself to believe
that i deserve less
than what i give
because past people
didn't have the capacity
to love me correctly

now i bury myself dizzy
in silk webbing
trying to remind myself
that thought is not fact

everything is so hard

i wish i could escape my mind
but it is forever running
quicker and quicker
until it catches up with my rationality;
a sprint that lunges into hysteria
and all the happy that makes me me
is now riddled with a sadness i cannot explain

and they tell me to cheer up
and i pretend to smile so that they
don't think i am ruining the time
and i do not want to be more of a burden
than i already feel that i am

so i play pretend
but inside this cancer debilitates my body
and i may have the energy to force
the corners of my lips upward today
but this heaviness may pin me
to my mattress tomorrow

and i try to tell myself that
this should be easy
getting up and walking
but inside i feel like i am decaying
spoiled fruit in the back of the fridge

this should be easy.
why is it not easy?

but i

i do not have trauma
because that would mean
i went to war

i did not have brothers die
in front of me
or deliver news to their families
along with attachments of apologies

and perhaps this is what is wrong
because i cannot imagine
the pain that is experienced;

a wound reopened
fresh
on a summer night
filled with colorful sky
kids on the hill laughing
lighting wicks

i do not have trauma
because i did not go to war
but i was raped last summer

hypocrite

we used to go
around and around in circles
while i would spit about accountability
or lack thereof
villainizing you for not meeting my needs
however this circle was more square
as i boxed you into a corner
made demands of you
knowing that you were not
capable of meeting them
but i chose to challenge [them] anyway.
maybe i was the toxic one

beauty standards

i feed words
tasting bitter of battery
to myself
charged with hatred and contempt
capitalized by industries
disguised in sheepskin
who possess wolfish fangs.
beauty is no longer in the eye
of the beholder
but lined in the pockets
of the rich

what resilience means to me

if i understand myself better
maybe i can heal it
all the trauma i've encountered
the idioms i've created
to relay messages of resiliency
but years after it happened
i gaslight myself
into thinking i am invalid
because others had it worse
now i hate
the word resilience
because it is not a compliment
but instead a justification
for things i should not
have endured
allow me to be soft
not hardened
by the idea
that i am defined
by this thing
called resilience

depression

i wish there was a medicine to cure
the voice that feeds my narrative
because i am waiting with patience
for myself to return to the train station
that i departed from
sometime in autumn
before the ache
seeped into the ground
but now it is winter and cold
and i am not me
and this is like war
while i wait to see if
i will ever return to myself

loudest

it is tiring to feel your bones heavy
your flesh shackled to the floorboards
knotted wood
knotted stomach
a hollowness that is not understood
unless one has heard
the deafening voice that asks
am i enough?
because my head is the loudest

paradox

my thoughts are cruel
when i want to be kind
but how can i be kind
when i hate myself?

performative

i am afraid to love
i romanticize the act
of falling
participate in the verb
but have woken
to realize
that it has been performative
love requires vulnerability
and i am no good at this
because if i share
how i feel
it will do nothing more
than scare you off
and i'd rather not
authentically love
just to authentically hurt
so i say the right things
do the right things
but close myself off
to the possibility
of connection.
it's the push and pull
of wanting more
but equally terrified
of losing it

self/after-care

sometimes all the self-care
in the world
won't fix the tired
that you feel
perhaps that's because
it's after-care
and you've been neglecting
yourself for too long

eaten away

maybe i lost pieces of myself
or maybe i left the womb
never being whole
not to the world
who believes i am worth nothing more
than what it can consume of me

nothing is wrong

i should bandage my feet
from the repetition
of tip-toe walking
never on eggshells
always razorblades
if i made myself small enough
maybe i would be too light
to obtain injury
but instead
i drip
drip
drip
blood
across the floor
mop it up with my feelings

imposter syndrome

i have a reoccurring nightmare
that i step outside my body
exit through my mouth
a sleeve i wear
and everyone can see that
i am a fraud

untitled 1

she filled her body
with the words whispered by men
because she felt nothing
and thought this would touch her insides.

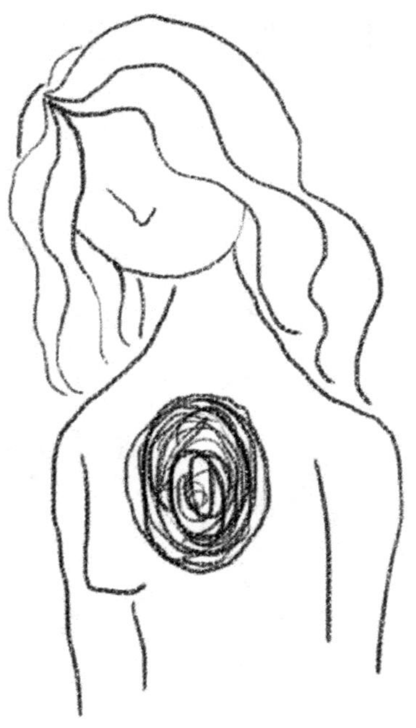

empty

some days i wish i were enough
because i've had enough
of not feeling like enough
a raw space
did i vacate this hole
or was it never filled?

script

i can't put into words
the feelings that i feel
knotted laces in my head
i wish to unstring
but i trip over them
every time you ask me
what is wrong
temporary amnesia
and i want to build closeness
but the script inside me
tells me that
everything i feel
is wrong
so wrong

untitled 2

sometimes i wish my mother
never parted her legs
so that i would not feel the pain
of being here
when here is too much

i am not meant to be loved

i beat myself
on repeat
hammer thoughts that become belief
that i am not good enough
to be chosen
perhaps i self-sabotage
because oh the devastation
i would experience
if i was surprised
that i was the placeholder
until the one i wanted
found the one he wanted

please come home

i have been tired for some time now
but while the world sleeps
i hang the sleeve of my body
out to dry
pinned to the taut line
hoping to feel aired by morning.

i am not the kind of tired
where rest will fix me though

no.

i am the kind where my
authenticity has been sleeping
a slumber of time that i cannot recall
because i am far away while
i let her wander
with the hopes that she will return
warm and alive

and though i am exhausted
and the bones in my body
that hold me upright
feel clunky in my skin
i modge podge a smile
and hope that it will beckon
her back to me.

and when the next person
asks how i am
and i say *i am fine. and you?*
i will wonder if they are tired too
are they waiting for themselves
to return as well?

deficient

i have never been in love
and often those feelings of butterflies
turned bats
beating against iron ribs
are less butterfly in nature
and more fleeing in anxiety

and perhaps that is what i've had
because every attempt to feel
has led me down a rabbit hole
waterboarded
red flags disguised as love
but yet red flags still

and often i dismiss,
allowing blood fabric
to turn into a blaring siren
until i am forced to question my ability
to select a healthy individual
one who will awaken me
from my fogged sleepwalk

i wish to have my nerves regulated, you see
not my senses heightened
am i deficient in the love hormone?
can something be prescribed?

or do i just not trust myself
and have yet to learn to lean into another
because i am trying
and trying
and should love feel so hard?
or am i?

i am not me

i do not recognize me
my voice sounds different
far away and muddy
like i am gurgling water
choking down salt
it stings my eyes
and burns my tongue
i'm trying to hold back the rain
of tears that stain my face
i do not recognize me
i wonder if anyone else does

i cannot trust

i have always found myself discarded
even when i know myself to be a rarity
a genuine treasure that is sought after
but yet he tossed me like trash
on the sidewalk
crumpled wrapper with empty insides

and i hate him for it
for making me feel less than
and unworthy of closure
just as i hate the man before him
and the man before the man

because i have known nothing more
than to give myself wholeheartedly
only to be met with
cruelty and carelessness
for my emotional being

i have felt too much
and been too little
for people who i have asked
the bare minimum from
and now i hate the men
who have made me question my worth
twisted my inner dialogue
because i am still perpetuating the fear
of not being enough

so though i know good men exist
with pure intentions
if i am greeted by a warm smile
my feet yet tell me
to run

because he always will

self-hate

i am mean
my mind utters words
that i would never speak to another
so why do i tell myself these things?

forgiveness is not easy

i have forgiven you
for taking me greedily
when you knew i had little
of myself to begin with
yet i offered you more
while i slowly became less
because i wanted to make you whole
but i have not forgiven myself
for draining myself empty

dissociative clutter

my home is messy
it resembles my head
a collection of things
that i just can't escape from

bitter

i am bitter
alkaline batteries to the tongue
because a man has ruined me
and i allowed it
so i am bitter
toward myself

to be needed

i find little satisfaction
in my own selfishness
i have always found myself to be the giver
even when i have nothing to offer
because who will need me
if i have come bearing empty hands?

funeral

i dig a hole
wide and deep
far down in the earth
where the hole can swallow everything
and i attend my own funeral
mourning the part of me
that has died

disposable

i am an avoider of things
things that are people
because one day i am their light
and the next day i am disposable

circles

wander and wander
and wonder if i will ever stop
trying to find myself
in other people.

mourning

they talk about how terrible
it is to lose someone
especially when it's untimely.
they grip memories
like choked snakes
the tighter they become
the more difficult it is
for them to wriggle away
and perhaps that is the
scariest part of this all
not necessarily losing a person
but losing the feelings of
what they meant to you
until they become a passing thought
that visits less and less frequently.
until sure enough, one day
they are forgotten entirely
almost as if that
person never existed:
a snake that wriggles free.
this is what my depression feels like
i don't remember me

self-medicating

i have been filling myself with people
because a part of me has been incomplete.
i have lost interest
in reconnecting with those pieces
that have been made soluble in
my hollowness
swallowed, perhaps,
is the better term.
i once had hope, you see
but it has become ungrounded
drifting off somewhere in the horizon
at dusk
and sadly, for me
there is only perpetual dusk
and i am standing squinted-eyed
at the edge of the dark
while my pupils dilate
to try to find this hope
so that i can reel it back in
with hook and pole
and build myself whole once more.
because filling myself with people
only provides temporary relief
to this numb
and i am tired of self-medicating

self-hatred

i poured myself
over and over
an endless spout of
lies that i spit between bared teeth
closed lips
fed from the inner
depths of my head
that tried to push me back into my box

with the tap still run
steady or drip
i spilled over the edges
until i became sopping wet sludge

you are nothing
my inner dialogue scorned
holy water run dirty
and i am fighting back
trying to drain this exhaustion
but it is replenished with more exhaustion

and i am afraid i will run
until the top of my head is filled
and what has made me me
is too diluted;

my lips pressed to the ceiling of my skull
to draw last breath
drowned

this is how i feel right now
this is self-hatred

spooled thoughts

i think myself into corners
loose thoughts strewn
in messy places
executing one task
while my mind wanders to
all the others
it would be a better use
of time
to think of the things
that made me good host
to anxiety's keeping
i'm working on that:
spooling my thoughts
so that i am happy
and not prisoner
to my own
musty head

for the healing

intermittent love

when you have never known love
it is difficult to recognize.
i've found it in people who perpetuate
the narrative that
love and hurt are interchangeable
yet it is universally desired.

it took me years to realize
that love does not hurt
and the two are separate in feeling
yes, one can hurt you and still love you
but others can hurt you and disguise this
as a character defect

do not soften at half-attempted apologies
given with motives of malice
to keep you coming back for more.
"i love you, but you made me do it."

and how dangerous it is
when you have never known love
and are taught that it
must be earned

you will long to hear those words
while your abuser dangles them
from his tongue
to see you beg

but darling
love and hurt are not synonymous

i am not a broken child

i have forgiven you
and that was the hardest thing
i've ever done.
i was supposed to be safe
and protected
and this was your one job
and you did your best
as you tell me that in the today
but it was not enough.
i was a child
and i had no voice
and when i spoke
i was silenced
into the corner
of my head that whispered
cruel things
because cruel things were done
and i have forgiven you
because i will not
continue to punish myself

name to a feeling

i hope one day that i find love
because i have been looking for it
as if it were something that i misplaced
but the trouble is
that i've never actually met it
so i tend to water it in people who give
a name to a feeling
and think because that person remembers
that minute detail about me
that it must be love
but this name can be any name
to a feeling, you see
and i've tried so hard to
mold that feeling into love
when perhaps it is a
deep longing and sadness
a complicated bereavement of sorts
for a death that i do not know.
so i attend a funeral
mourne the potential of a love
that could be grown if conditions were right
but all i've ever known is conditional:
conditional attention
and conditional praise
conditional affection
and conditional love
and let me tell you
that is not love.
so yes, i hope one day i find it
and if i cannot find that love in someone
then i wish to at least find it in myself

heavy

i know that some days feel heavy
and some of those days
turn into weeks
and other weeks are months
and at times, it feels endless
you have begun to forget what excites you
have you not?
because the world is moving
and you feel still
but not the kind of still that
has you in awe
but the kind where your own
limbs feel foreign
and you are seeing but it is
not with your own eyes
and everything is heavy
oh so heavy.
have you forgotten what it
feels like to be you?
don't worry
you will return

my worth is more

i am not too much
for asking to be loved
in the way that i love

i do not accept room temp
interest that is led to spoil
because someone did not want
to preserve my shelf life

i am not too needy
for longing for your words
or touch
when you have withheld that
in an attempt to wither me

and i am not too loud
for telling you that your
lack of effort makes me
feel unwanted and unseen

and i am surely not
too difficult for upholding boundaries
something that took me so long to learn
practice after practice
to get right
despite what you twist

so today i am walking away
because this no longer serves me

uninspired

i look for inspiration
to write about you
so that i do not lose feelings
i think if i were to stop feeling
i would forget you
and there is nothing more terrifying
than you becoming ordinary
your birthday just another day
i ask the stranger
the date
and my mind doesn't wander to you.
you do not occupy room in my head
and as the days pass
you take up less and less space
my life goes on
until i never think of you again.
i look for inspiration
to write about you
so you are not forgotten

lovers to roommates

i am not scared of losing you

no.

i am scared of living in a
dead-end relationship
in which we dance around
the mutual feeling
that this is not what
we want anymore
and that is okay

we are allowed to
change our minds
and we are allowed to
outgrow each other
while we search for our own
separate meanings

it does not mean that
i do not love you
but backs turned
toward each other
on a springy mattress
pretending that feelings
are as they were
is not appealing anymore

i do not want to play house
which now holds empty:
silent mornings as we shuffle
around the kitchen
bare feet on linoleum
spewing coffee machine
filling the quiet
between us

we once had a vision for us as a whole
and now we have realized
without acknowledgement
that we have run our course

i will still love you
i promise
but i will love you
as the setting of sun right now
knowing i will see
another orange sky
but never the same one

5 stages of losing yourself

i thought i had lost you
and i went through all the
stages of grief
it was so slow—your death
almost as if it never happened

and i denied your absence
convinced it was rooted in deceit
still waiting for the magician
to pull you from his
black top hat

i was angry when i called to you
pick up, i need you
a rage that i did not understand because
one day you were here and the next
you were gone

maybe if i called back
at a time when you were done resting
i would hear your voice
because i was not used to my head being

so quiet.
so empty.

did you move out
without saying goodbye?

i whispered to you hushed
come back to me
pleaded on bruised knees
until they became raw
from kissing the ground
don't leave me
i'll love you harder this time

it was then that i experienced
a sadness that
clouded the forefront of my mind
i cannot move because
i do not know how to
without you
and i am here
but so far away
somehow we became untethered

and i thought that when i had
accepted that you were gone
perhaps forever
that i would feel better
mostly, i did not

i grieved every bit of you, you see
turned you over in my palms
and i still think of you some days;
wonder if you will
ever return to me

but i realized you died
so that i could birth
myself out of my own discomfort
did you plant yourself
in the ground i kissed
so that i could bloom anew?

i should be grateful
but i still miss you

i will speak

they duct tape my mouth so that
i do not speak out of turn
in a society that believes
my voice is lesser
so i await my turn patiently
listening to words that
make my insides burn
a wretched fire that fuels my being
little do they know
i possess scissors
so i snip the tape

an apology to myself

dear self,
i am sorry that i did not hold you
when the scared child inside
needed to be held
i am sorry that i betrayed you
like all the others that have spit lies
dressed as flowers
plucked from deceit and
bound by false twine
i have abandoned you
when you needed me
i have dismissed your feelings
as being too much
i have run away from you
like all the others
and fed you conditional lies
to bruise your flesh
but i am here now
please forgive me
i promise i will
never leave you again

you are worthy

someday you will not need to
beg him to stay
you will not cry for him
to love you right
because he will know
what to do with the gift
you've presented
your soul wrapped in a red bow
dressed in gloss
because the right man
will recognize your value
even before he has
unwrapped your flesh

serve yourself

child,
you are hurting over a person
who you did not truly know.
this does not make your hurt less valid
but let me remind you that
potential is not what you are seeking
you are strong
and brave
and gentle
and you wear authenticity like a garnish
attracting souls that are wounded
seeking shelter in the genuine.
and it is beautiful to be a calm
to those who have been at
war with themselves
but it is not your job to
dismantle the bomb
that they have left intact
in their back pocket.
it is not your job
to trust them
not to weaponize their words or
love them through their sabotage.
you need not obliterate yourself to
serve another
and let me remind you of
what you are owed
trusting that you will recognize
when this is no longer serving you

more

i am more
than a collection of words
adjectives that are strung
across the forefront of your mind
when you think of me
you think of my body
how it splits for you
cracks like wood
how my spine curves
arching as you part my legs
you think i'm beautiful
but i am so much more

darkness, my friend

turn off the lights
not because the dark will swallow you
but because you will not know
the feeling of sun
until you have become friends
with night

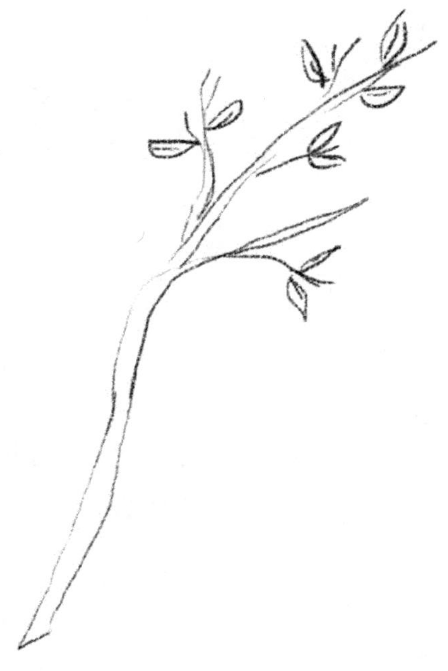

my name

call me by my name
because there is no word
to describe me
so when you call me beautiful
it doesn't ring true
because i am more

moving through it

i let grief turn to rain
it trickles down my skin
drips from tip of nose
and pools at my feet
though i am made of water
i will not become grief
just allow myself to feel it
a necessary
in order to move through it

puddles

you deserve the ocean
not mud puddles
created by rain clouds
of tears
although those puddles may ripple
and resemble movement
disguised as love,
you deserve tidal waves
something strong
not something broken
by breeze

i am getting there

i have always been half-empty
carrying a shell
of armor that is meant
to protect my outer skin
because i have not yet learned
the art of growing scales
so that your arrows do not
puncture my flesh
but today
i will teach myself
the beauty of growth

healing

i have had my heart broken
stomped on flat
and thrown against a wall to shatter
but i will be okay
because my cracks will be
filled with gold
kintsugi

societal standards

i was not made for this world
i am convinced
because this world is about
symmetry
and shape
and size
my worth has been
reduced to a number
that clings to my waist
my breasts
measurements that in/validate
my existence
but when i look at another
i see into them
are you kind?

try again later, or not at all

if my body offends you
just know
it does not need your permission
to simply exist.

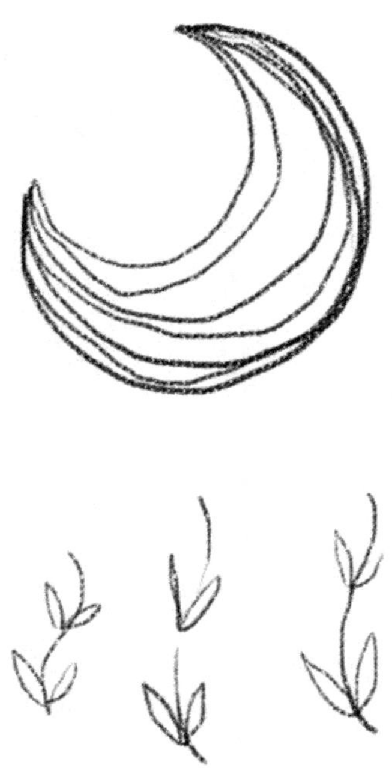

wild

i am a creature of the night
born in the quiet
but if you listen closely
there is a choir of crickets
a collection of howls and yowls
a movement of reaching branches
that crackle with the
whip of the wind
do not mistake my quiet
as a resting place
because my mind still runs wild

full

i wish to be loved gently
i do not need rocky instability
half in-half out
because i know my worth
and it is a love that is full
not half

i get to choose too

i spent so much of my time
fixating on whether or not you liked me
that i began to lose sight of who i was.
things that made up my identity
became diluted
so that i would become more digestible.
perhaps you have a sensitive stomach
but watering myself down
was not the antidote.
i mirrored you
so that i could be your medicine
and was so focused on making you
like me
fixing your flaws
that i needed to step back for a moment.
i began to shift this overthinking dialogue
to my inner voice
do i even like you?

bandaged with cayenne

i have been talking to myself unkindly
criticizing my perception of others
punishable by self-hatred
for choices they made
that ultimately had little to do with me

i have thought that perhaps if i didn't love so hard
i would hurt less

if i were slower to trust
i would have seen that they would
manipulate my feelings
with their ill intentions
and i could have avoided death
both at the hand of them and
by my own harshness

i have thought that it was their deliberation
to inflict wounds upon me
lick them clean with salt
bandaged with cayenne

but this is what my inner voice has told me
and after reflection
i have demanded this voice to

just.

shut.

up.

i have realized that these people
were wounded too
and that perhaps their
intentions were not so ill after all

and in fact, they simply couldn't
love me back
not because they didn't want to
but because their inner voice echoed
unkindly things to them as well

no answer

i have learned to question everything
because i can live with
a question with no answer
but it is dangerous
to live with an answer
that is not questioned

cold mornings

cold winter mornings
frost lace on the window glass
warm coffee cupped in hands
steam swirling in air
i blow comfort into the mug
this time last year i thought
i would never make it through
a day without
grieving the loss of you
our lives untethered
today i am fine
i sit on the couch
stare out at the
blanket of fresh snow
i made it

pearls to rope

your words were stung pearls
worn around my neck
beautiful and elegant
until the clasp pulled tight
tight, tight clasp
and i choked
your words now twisted rope
as i hang limp
but i cut myself free
that is what it is like
to break away from your tormenter

i'm okay

i used to fill my time
with the company of men
because you did not want me
i thought i could find you
in the skin of others
my ex-lover
but now i fill my time
with the company of my own head
because it is now tranquil here
and i don't remember
your phone number
by heart

poems

i reflect on dog-eared pages
of poems that reminded me
of the heartbreak
i felt when we ended
now i read poems
of healing because
i am nearly finished

no longer yours

i still have your sweater
the one with the ash hole in the sleeve
you never smoked
maybe touch burned hot
singed a hole
and i wear it still
but never think of you

breaking patterns

i scale buildings
for the thrill of the jump
i romanticize the freefall
wind whipping hair up
as i suspend in time
how it is to create
false intimacy
because i want someone
to love me
but midfall
i realize i can catch myself

bats and wasps

the birds and the bees
were bats and wasps
i know enough
to know that i was blinded
by your potential
convinced myself that
you were all i needed
but never again
will i abandon myself
for damp caves of hope
and stingers

reminder

i looked in the bottom drawer
of my nightstand
i've avoided it for three years
i know there are photographs of us
and i can't bring myself
to discard them.
i used to think it
was because i loved you
but it's because i love me
and they remind me
of nothing i will
ever put up with again

feel my way through

don't be dramatic
i tell myself
knees to chest
resemblance of a tight ball
heavy
someone has been sitting on me.
this will pass
and i force myself to feel
my way through
the sorrow
so that i can shed skin
to the healed person
beneath

permission to self

i do not need to know
who i am today
there is a pressure
of certainty
if i do not know now
i must be lost
it is okay to bump
into feelings
and thoughts
and people
and to let it play out
until i find myself

validation

i used to dress myself
in appealing attire
to flatter a man
into believing i was a great catch
let me boast
overshare
pay attention to me
because i was trying
to convince myself
that i was worthy
so i focused on being perfect
for him
and did not care
but for one thing:
being validated
now i have done my own work
with the glorious realization
that the validation
comes from me

what i value

i have learned
from hard life lessons
that the world
will not give me
preferential treatment
for being good
it does not hold moral
value like people do
no.
but these same life lessons
have taught me
that i do not want to be
without feeling
because what a shame it would be
to not love life enough
to be anything
but kind

with the current

i'm learning to move
through my feelings
no longer upstream
it is okay
there are no wrong ones
so let me float
with the current
until i arrive
where i'm
supposed to be

my feelings matter

i cared so much about
your feelings
i thought it
would be enough for two
to the point where if
i brought something up
that upset me
i'd give first aid
to your ego
and abandon my
own emotions
i thought it was selfless
but each time i learned
to feel less
so all that was left
was myself
thank you for teaching me
to never do that again

pressure to [immediately] answer

i don't want to be
codependent
i cannot talk to you
all the time
because i gave every second
to him
so that he and i
became chain-linked.
i'd never felt less
like my own person
than when his words
turned to shackles
buzz buzz
answer now.
i don't want to be
codependent
so let's take it slow

cycle breaker

i give myself a medal
for not becoming
the person that
generational trauma
wanted me to be

i will choose softness

i will not allow myself
to harden
i will not put on armor
to wage internal wars for
past mistakes
i made as i was learning
to love myself whole
i wasn't kind to you
and i apologize
i promise not to lick razorblades
to taste harm
and further self-destruct
you deserve softness
not more punishment
for choosing people
who chose to hurt you